WISE...

BEYOND HER YEARS

Collected Poems 1972 - 1980

Sybil Ingram, PhD.

To all those teens out there with stifled voices about their real feelings – the pen and paper are always there, ready to tenderly and patiently 'hear' your voice and express your true feelings, unapologetically.

CONTENTS

Make Up Your Mind — 3
Little Boy Blue — 5
Ode to Ultra-Sheen — 7
Nursery Rhymes — 8
Sweet Young Delicacy — 10
Sittin' By the Telephone — 12
Grace — 13
Life is Just a Ball — 14
I Don't Need You Because I Can Exist Without You — 16
All I Need — 17
I Regret with Deepest Sympathy… — 18
I Am Me — 19
Black People Are Funny Sometimes — 21
If I Was to Say to You that I Love You — 24
In Times Past — 26
Lullaby — 28
Interlude — 30
You 'n Me — 31
Sybil's Creed — 33
Jesus — 37
We Got New Lights on Our Block Now — 39
Like a Lady — 41
King Heroin — 43
The Stiff-legged Man — 45
We've Got a Band — 47
The Conductor — 48
Let My Love In — 49

ACKNOWLEDGMENTS

I couldn't have done with without Kim from NewFrontierBooks.com – she's the bomb. Thank you for believing in me, my words, and how these poems cross through the decades.

Thank you to Cynthia Stoud for typing up my handwritten poems. Your hard work deciphering my handwriting helped bring this book into reality.

And thank you to the people, the era, the circumstances that inspired me to write these poems. Your impact on me will impact many others.

MAKE UP YOUR MIND

With all your complications and your intricacies,
you're found to be fascinating, especially to me.

You're oh, so very wonderful, and yet you're hard and mean.
You've got the evilest evil streak that I have ever seen.

You're so very antagonizing, but I've got the patience to deal.
You could be considered sadistic, and at times, so very unreal.

I'd like to come to know you, but you give me an ice-wall stance.
I'd like to become a part of you if you'd give me just a chance.

At times, I'm mad about ya. At times, I hate your guts.
My emotions about you are so erratic, till I feel I'm going nuts.

I've never met a person quite exactly like you.
The reality of your existence is too phenomenal to be true.

Your megalomaniac attitude is more than I can take.
Your childish little games waste time and cause my heart to break.

Your mannerisms are cold and more than I care to bear.
I'm staying to stick it out, 'cause I've got a lot I want to share.

I've got a lot that you should have. I've got a lot that you should
        need.
I've got a lot that you could learn. Just don't make me have to
        plead.

Your arrogance is unnecessary. You oughta drop that mask of
        yours.

Your insignificant insecurities I could substitute with something
    more.

You haven't blown my mind, but you've wasted some of my time.
I'd like to know where I stand before I call you my main man.

I'd like to know real cool if you are to be my fool?
I'd like to know right fast how long you expect me to last.

I'd love to be your one and only. I'd like to think that's true.
I'd like to know where I stand. I wanna hear it from you.

If I am just a friend, that'll be all right with me.
At least I'll be released of this unnecessary misery.

MAKE UP YOUR MIND.
DON'T WASTE MY TIME.
DON'T WASTE YOUR TIME.
MAKE UP YOUR MIND.

May 3, 1976

LITTLE BOY BLUE

Little Boy Blue,
where are you?
'Cause I'm feeling your color.

Blow me a tune that I'll remember,
with the passing of
a life's time,
my life's time.

Little Boy Blue,
don't be shy.
Show yourself and get down!

Get down with your melodic tunes,
concocted uniquely by you,
for its time to share (if you dare)
what you've got, with one
who could use your gift of escapism.
For granting liberty to a burdened, troubled mind and soul.
One who calls upon you!

Little Boy Blue,
blow me a tune.
'Cause I'm feeling your color.

Blow me a tune and release one
from these barbarous thoughts.
From these menacing perspectives.
From these torturous ideologies.

Release one into your harmonic world of blissful renaissance.
Let one become absorbed and feel

at peace with one's thoughts.
Permit one to tap to your beat for a while...if you dare...
if you care...
if you're true.

Little Boy Blue,
blow me a tune.
'Cause I'm sholly feeling your color.

June 10, 1977

ODE TO ULTRA-SHEEN

On this page of green,
I dedicate to Ultra-Sheen.
Ultra-Sheen, Ultra-Sheen,
a hair product that's blue,
Ultra-Sheen, Ultra-Sheen,
I love you.

You manage my hair so wonderfully,
And keep it looking lov-el-ly.
Ultra-Sheen, Ultra-Sheen,
A product that's not new,
But any ole way,
I remain in love with you.

If this page is white,
I'd write about a fight.
If this page was red,
I'd write about a bed.
If this page was yellow,
I'd write about a mighty fine fellow.
If this page was grey,
I'd write about night and day.
If this page was pink,
I'd write about the kitchen sink.
If this page was blue,
I'd dedicate it to you.
But since this page is green,

I dedicate it to Ultra-Sheen.

June 6, 1973

NURSERY RHYMES

Hickory, Dickory,
jump on in!
Crying in a world
that's dying in sin.

Pease porridge hot!
I'm getting cold.
Trying to live a life
that's already been foretold.

Rub-a-dub-dub!
I'm in a sub.
Trying to look out and see myself,
my life,
my values,
my priorities,
fluctuating in front of me.

Hey Diddle-Diddle!
Stuck in the middle!
Wondering who it could be?
Crashing through blockades
of obstructive constructions,
searching for self-identity.

Hickory Dickory Dock.
Tick Tock, Tick Tock.
This damn clock
just won't stop.
My head, I hear it.
My eyes, I see it.
My breath, I feel it.

My heart, I'm losing it.
My time, running out of it,
Tick Tock.
Tick Tock.

June 10, 1977

SWEET YOUNG DELICACY

Sweet, young delicacy,
waiting to be savored.
Succulent and richly spiced.
Abundant in amount.
Infinitely provided for, too!

Seek your special herb and spice,
to add to your ever-so-tempting dish.
Seek not too far though,
For it is very near and is it ready!

Ripe and taunt as you can imagine,
raw and pure in form,
waiting to be used by you,
teased by you,
cared by you.

Handle it carefully!
Wash and caress it well.
It's just what you need
to accent yourself.
It's that missing ingredient
that you've looked for so long.
The one that finally makes your
dish complete,
and, umph, too much!

It's complementary.
It's free.
It's destined to be!
It's your added attraction.
So people will come,

far and near,
to take part of yourself.

But...you're greedy,
possessive,
selfish, and conceited.

No one but you and the extra
will know how you taste.
They'll be missing the event of their lives,
to partake of such an entrée.

You don't care.
You like it this way
(so does extra).
You sweet, young, succulent thing!

(Blessed be your creator. He/She outdid themselves this time.)

December 1977

SITTIN' BY THE TELEPHONE

Sittin' by the telephone,
waiting for a phone call.
Looks like I'm not going to get one
after all.

In the inner channels of my mind,
a beat is kept in time.
"I'm just a sucker for your love.
For your love, for your love."

GRACE

By the grace of God,
we are all brought here today.
By the grace of God,
throughout tormented eons of ages,
we still exist.
This Grace,
which no one can feel,
touches us all,
at one time or another,
if we let it.
Like God,
it's sender,
it comes in various forms.
Taking on various shapes.
Grace comes to all who allow it to come to them,
like anything else.
May the Grace of God be with us always,
for we shall, and continue to be,
needy of the Grace that is bestowed upon us.
Time and time again,
to let us carry on his work,
by the Grace of God.

January 17, 1975

LIFE IS JUST A BALL

Listen, honey, I'm okay,
because it's a new day.
And nothing, no nothing, can bother me anyway.

I've been pushed around like
someone's clown.
I don't want to be knocked down.

Life is just a ball that goes
around,
but I'm sick and tired of you
putting me down.

Let me go out
and find myself.
Because you don't care for
no one else.

Life is just a jet
that zooms and flies.
Every time I tell the truth, I get
nothing but lies.

Listen, honey, I'm
leaving you.
What we had is
long gone through.

Life is just a top that
whirls and spins.
Look, I don't want to hear no more.
Oh,

here we go again.

I'm going to find myself with
another kind.
No more do I want to
blow your mind.

Life's a ball and top
and yet a jet.
But listen, just listen, cause
you ain't seen nothing yet.

March 18, 1973

I DON'T NEED YOU BECAUSE I CAN EXIST WITHOUT YOU

I don't need you,

because I can exist without you,
but ...
my day,
my time,
my life
goes better,
flows better,
with you in my day,
my life,
my time.

Your presence makes that much of a difference in
my day,
my life, my time.

You are much needed,
much wanted,
and very much loved.

1980

ALL I NEED

No one to live for,
no one to die for,
but someone to love.
That's all I need.

No one to lie for,
no one to stick up for,
but someone to care for.
That's all I need.

No one to steal for,
no one to fight for
but someone to trust.
That's all I need.

No one to laugh with,
no one to cry with,
but someone to share with.
Could you be what I need?

July 9, 1973

I REGRET WITH DEEPEST SYMPATHY...

I regret,
with deepest sympathy,
that while I was president,
nothing got accomplished.
Except
voting on new uniforms
and another bake sale.
Man...

I AM ME

In these dim moments of strife,
I can clearly see my life
stretched out farther than it can be.
But more and more, I can see,
I, as a proud one, a Black one.
That's a fact,
ready and willing to try.
Now run and tell that.
Ready to make the world see that
I am me.

Don't tell me who I was or who I am.
Don't tell me I'm gentle as a lamb.
Cause I'm NOT!
I'm Fierce!
Militant
and Free!
But most of all,
I Am Me.

I'll come on stronger than a lion.
Yeah, I'll keep on trying.
So fast!
I'll not back down to anyone I get.
But listen, cause you ain't seen nothing yet.
And I'll soon make you believe
and see.
I am me.

I plea to my brothers and sisters
not to fall.
I call to them together,

one, two, all.
To help me fight and establish
our role,
to bring to this world love, peace, and soul.
Then we shall make them see,
with Thee at our hand,
that... I am me!

December 28, 1972

BLACK PEOPLE ARE FUNNY SOMETIMES

You Know,
Black People Are Funny Sometimes.
Some try to go out to get equal opportunity jobs for Blacks after
        300 years being Emancipated.
And You Notice,
The person who is usually running off at the jibs about freedom
        has a list of Flunkies to his name.

You Know,
Black People Are Funny Sometimes.
Take the dope pusher, for instance.
He gets into the racket when things are going sorta bad for him.
And Then You Notice,
as soon as he gets together, he wants to pull out.
Like the saying goes,
"When the going gets tough, the Tough get Going."

You Know,
Blacks Are Funny Sometimes.
They can find something funny to laugh about
even at the lowest of times.
And You Notice,
some big shots will give large sums of money to organizations for
        under-privileged, depressed people.
But if one of these depressed people who the Big Shot gave the
        money to come up to the Big Shot for more money, he
        will more than likely get on the person's case and knock
        him out of the way.
I guess the funds didn't come in fast enough.

You Know,
Black People Are Funny Sometimes.

A lot of them talk loud, but say anything.
And You Notice,
most of them who have the answer
evidently never heard the question.

You Know,
Black People Are Funny Sometimes.
They love to preach about how good they can cook and have la-
          beled it "Soul Food."
And You Notice,
most of the people who rap the loudest about it
usually turns out to be a very un-together person.

You Know,
Black People Are Funny Sometimes.
When most of them get money,
the first thing they do is spend it on a lot of junk or give it to their
          church.
Not that there's anything wrong with giving money to the
          church.
But You Notice,
The person who shouts the loudest,
and gives the most amount of money on Sunday,
is usually the one winning all the money at the racetrack on Satur-
          day night.

You Know,
Black People Are Funny Sometimes.
Everybody's talking about your Sickle Cell Anemia and lead poi-
          soning test 'fo we all wiped off de face of de earf'.
And You Notice,
The biggest and the baddest talker is the one to strut boldly into
          the doctor chair, roll up his sleeve, and pass out at the
          sight of a needle.

You Know,
Black People Are Funny Sometimes.
Winos seem to live a happy, gay life
and hope when they fall down, their red wine in their back
          pocket, its blood.
And You Notice,
The person who usually makes a big deal about going on a vaca-
          tion

comes back talking about the city, just as calmly as if he had lived there all the time.

June 1973

IF I WAS TO SAY TO YOU THAT I LOVE YOU

If I was to say to you that I truly do,
If I was to say to you that I love you,
Would you love me too?

If I was to say to you that I love you,
If I was to love you for all time,
If I was to say to you that I love you,
Would you become mine?

Time is so precious,
Too precious for us to waste.
Since love has come to us,
Let's lavish its taste.

If I was to say to you that I love you,
If I promised you a girl or a son,
If I was to say to you that I love you,
Would you be my one and only one?

If I was to say to you that I love you,
If I was to make for you a proud wife,
If I was to say to you that I love you,
Would you love me for life?

We've got to be together,
If we want to survive.
I love you madly as no other,
In love with you for the rest of our lives.

If I was to be your lady fair,
If I was to say to you that I love you,
Do you think you could really care?

(So, I'm going to say, HEY!)
I clearly love you!
I love you through and through.
Now I've got just one question.
What am I going to do?

I just can't bear living without you.

Life seems less important
With each fleeting moment.
With you, I mean something.
Without you, I mean nothing.

You've come into my life
And have stolen my heart.
Now it's breaking, hurting,
Because we're so far apart

We've got to be together
In everlasting love forever,
I'll always love you, my fine brother.
Like you, I'll never love another.

We've made our pact, our very deep promise,
To each other, my friend,
To love each other and cherish each other,
Until the very end.

April 4, 1975

IN TIMES PAST

In times past, ere, young and old,
you have come for me to behold.

Day and night become as one,
rising under some new-found sun,
enwrapping all within its embraces,
spewing forth love on camouflaged faces.

Faces amid a wondrous land,
one that transcends plain, mortal man.

One unknown to you and I
yet, one destined for us to try to find,
in our own way
and time.
Together,
with your hand in mine.

Together, with your hand in mine,
we'll race through heavens
far and near
until we reach that land, my dear.
Until we gasp for breath as one
and see the rise of new-found sun.
For us to watch with child-like eyes,
and pray and hope it never dies.
To watch it zenith again and again,
to us its mysteries will lend.

For us to feel as none before,
seething through each other's inner core,
wanting more and more and more,

as only, we only, could adore.

Oh! This our world of yet to be,
this our world of you and me.
In this world, filled with total bliss,
known to us through that tattle-tale kiss,
we'll venture in and out its door,
returning for more and more and more,
as two have never lusted before,
wanting more and more and more.

Being temporarily satisfied at each rendezvous,
you wanting me as I wanting you.
In succulent form, thine essence, divine!
For, my thoughts, floating,
brings only you to mind.

For me transcending,
bring you to me,
as mine.

LULLABY

Cree, cree,
Novice cree.
Cree, cree, my love,
Cree on, cree.

Don't let your mind
Waste all your time.
Cause you don't know
Which way to go.

Cree, cree,
Novice cree.
Cree, cree, my love,
Cree on, cree.

Cree, cree,
Novice cree.
Call up above,
Cree on, cree.

See the stars
Twinkle, twinkle.
Cree, cree my love,
Cree on, cree.

I call to One
Who hears my plea.
Cree, cree, my love,
Cree on, cree.

To hear my lament,
My wailing cry,

Cree, cree my love,
Cree on, cree.

Then a voice so soft
And sweetly,
Cree, cree my love,
Cree on, cree.

Beckons, beckons, beckons, beckons.

"I am here!
Have no fear!"
Cree, cree my love,
Cree on, cree.

"All your days,
Filled with joy and gladness.
No more days of
Tears and sadness.
Let your heart
Resound the heavens
Always, eternally, on and on and...

Cree, cree,
Novice cree,
Cree, cree my love,
Cree on, cree.

My little one,
Come unto me.
Cree, cree my love,
Cree on, cree.

Listen
For you'll always be free.
Cree, cree, my love,
Cree on, cree.

Have hope in your heart,
A song in your soul,
And you'll live on and on and on and...

January 1, 1974

INTERLUDE

So inspiring
and enlightening,
yet intriguing and hypnotic.
As the musician waves his baton
to conduct the orchestra.
He bobs.
He weaves.
He is in full control.
l sway to the beat of his command!

1984

YOU 'N ME

Say my friend, I know a man
who talks about a foreign land.
And that man, from way up there, says,
"Savoir-faire is everywhere."

Could it be, could it be,
you 'n me, yes, you 'n me.
Like savoir-faire, way up there
everywhere, yea everywhere.

We could be, just you and me,
in a tree, yea, in a tree,
or way up high in a cloud,
in the sky singing very loud.
Or in a dream, on some cream,
made of mesh, and very fresh.

You 'n me, yea you 'n me.
Oh how happy we could be!
Oh so free, so very free,
you 'n me, just you 'n me.

We could get in touch with that man
to take use to that foreign land.
And tell him there, to savoir-faire,
to take us every, everywhere.

Just you 'n me, you and me.
Oh how happy we could be,
totally free, just you and me.
Oh how happy we could be.

Get on a boat, there were not fees,
and sail us cross the seven seas.
Take us through crannies and niches,
and tell us tales of untold riches.
Where the sands are white as rice,
and oh, so very, very nice!
Where they sparkle like diamonds and glisten,
and siren's call for all to listen.
Where we would feast on nectar and honey,
and all the time so very sunny.
Then finally, at last, alone,
you 'n me in our sweet new home.
we'll walk along, hand-in-hand,
Together in our new-found land.
You 'n me, you 'n me.
Oh how happy we could be!
Just you 'n me, you 'n me,
totally free, just you 'n me.

We'll walk along
without a care in the world,
you the boy and I the girl.
Time is ours, no days or hours,
and watch the moon, while it will rise,
and speak with nothing 'cept with our eyes,
and reminisce from time to time,
sipping on un-soured wine.
Together till the dawn of day,
and loving every moment in every way.
And never parting, no never, not never,
eternal love forever and ever.

You 'n me, you 'n me.
Oh how lovely it would be!
You 'n me, just you 'n me,
Totally free,
just you 'n me.

October 1, 1974

SYBIL'S CREED

I am Sybil.
I am bad, I am mad,
I am free, I am me.
I am hard, I am bold.
I'm together, and very cold.

I want to be in on a lot of things.
To be the first and the best means a lot to me.

I am a one and only, never to be seen on the face of this earth
        again.

I am one of a kind.
There will never be another Ms. Sybil Louise Ingram.

That's a fact.

While I am here,
I will let myself be known to all
who come in contact with me.
I will not be forgotten,
because I will not let myself be forgotten.

I'll turn into your shadow,
just so you'll remember that I was and still am here.
Death will not put an end to my work,
to what I had accomplished while I was alive.
My believers, my followers, my partners,
my friends, my brothers and my sisters,
will carry me on.

I am hot,

ready to explode like a volcano
with hot lava exploding forth from my every action.

I'm an atom bomb.
Push my trigger, my button, my plunger,
and there you are.

I am unstoppable.
I am positive.
I have sheer determination.
I soon will be a deadly weapon to all who cross my path.

I am black.
I am very proud.
I have regal esteem for myself.

I am cunning as a fox, sly as a panther, and deadly as a cobra.

I have qualities no average person has,
simply because I am not an average person.
I have unlimited kinetic and potential power.

I have life, I have liberty,
and I demand justice for me and my fellow man.

I love as no one could love,
hate as no one could hate.
I feel as no one could feel.

I heal and help as no one could heal and help.
I destroy as no one could destroy.

I have the utmost respect for myself.
My imperial arrogance comes on strong to those who know me.

I hold nothing back.

I am for real.
I am a down-to-earth person.
All my cards are laid out on the table for all to see.

I hide nothing but take a lot.

My satirical wit is much too much for some to handle.

My angered temper ranges to a very high,
incomparable, uncontrollable, uncouth state of mind or being.

I've got to get into the system, learn the rules, make the rules.
I've got to get a lot of inside information on a vast majority of im-
portant factors.

I am my own hit squad.

I love to be independent and carefree,
for I could care less about a vast majority of unimportant topics,
subjects of interest

to those with little or scrutinizing minds. I hate chains or bonds.
I despise over-protecting authority.

I've got to be on the case at all times, constantly on the defense
24-hours a day, 7-days a week, 365 days a year.
Letting down my guard could ruin me.
I will not let myself be wiped out by anything or anyone.
If some ignorant, unsuspecting sucker dares cross me, woe be to
him.
I'm not an easy catch. I'll give hell to anyone and everyone.

Because I am regular hell-raiser.

I've got to be strong. I've got to be direct.
My qualities must shine through, get projected over in my every
action.

I'm rough and tough. Full of action, suspense, excitement and ad-
venture.
Ready and willing to give you a run for your money anytime.

Hell yeah, I am bold.

It's about time you, and
everyone else, woke up and realized that fact.

Cold, despicable, inscrutable, unspeakable, and unbelievable bold-
ness
that comes through every time and has not failed me yet.

My day will come.
My day will come for revenge.
I've got spunk.
I've got ingenuity.

Most of all, I got guts.

I've got so much to back me up.
I've got so much going for me.
Why should I let some unknown sucker knock me off?
Hell yeah, I'm psyched up with hell, revenge, hate, scorn, destruc-
        tion.
You would, too, if you had to be me.

People make me, made me what I am.
I'm just improving the basis of their work to my ability
and turning the tables on them.
I've got room for love and happiness,
but not until all of my scores are settled.
Not until all my records are set straight with
me,
myself,
and I.

December 26, 1973

JESUS

Jesus is coming again;
the problem is when.
People call,
"Jesus, Jesus, come on, man.
Get us into the promised land!
Jesus, man, you said you'd come again,
but hey, man, you never exactly said when."

Jesus was born; he lived until his end.
Jesus even died for those who sin.
Jesus, came back, so say the brave.
Jesus came back from his cold, frosty grave.
Jesus resurrected for us all.
Jesus said he'd pick us up when we fall.
Jesus is one with the Father and the Holy Spirit.
Jesus has a call, but very few hear it.
Very few follow his golden rule,
and if you don't, you're considered a fool.
You get talked about, harassed, over and over.
These people really need a four-leaf clover.
But these people don't use it;
if they did, they'd share it with us.

Cause these people are firm believers in this man, Je-sus.
These believers put their all in JC.
They're sure he's coming again
to bring peace love and joy to all his believers.
So be it, all right, Amen.
So, if you're a believer,
you'll know exactly when
your Savior, Jesus,
is coming again.

If you're a true believer,
you'll know exactly when
your Savior, Jesus Christ,
is coming again.

WE GOT OUR NEW LIGHTS ON OUR BLOCK NOW

They're being put up all over the city;
they're supposed to help cut down on crime.

Crime.

Its rates soaring higher and higher,
mounting on top of each other into endless infinity.
When will it ever cease?
Will it ever cease?

Rapes, muggings, assaults, armed robberies
headline our newspapers,
day in and day out.
Now crime statistics piling upon each other,
filling our papers worth 15 cents.

Crime and murders
committed 24 hours a day, 7 days a week, 365 days a year.
When will it ever cease?
Will it ever cease?

"Wage a war against crime."
"Get involved," the people cry in anguish and despair.
"Get them before they get you! Who knows?
Their next victim may be you or a loved one."

Statements, slogans like this are repeated time after time again,
in a futile manner,
in a bewildered state of mind.

Some are moved to get involved.
Some take a very positive attitude towards the whole thing.
"Let's get it together," they say.
Some take a very negative view towards the whole thing.
"Oh, what the hell," they say.

We've got new lights.
Will their purpose in being here be fulfilled or
just another wasted product of our hard-earned money?

One thing for sure...
be it the brightest lights,
be it the most outstanding police force,
be it the most intelligent FBI agency,
crime will always still be there.
Lurking in every ditch,
waiting around every corner.
When will it all cease?
Will it ever cease?

Get involved! Get it together!
Who knows?
Maybe, just maybe next time, it could be you!
Take note. Contemplate. Think about it,
then get into action.
We've got the brain power,
the intellectual know-how.
Use it, then!
Get up off your _ _ _ and use it.

Time's running out and...

The lights can't do it all by themselves, baby!

December 16, 1974

LIKE A LADY

When you walk like a lady and you talk like a lady, and
you weep like a lady, and you sleep like a lady, and
you cry like a lady, and you sigh like a lady,
then you know that you are grown.

When you dance like a lady,
make romance like a lady,
bob your hair like a lady,
use some Nair like a lady,
do your nails like a lady,
prim and frail like a lady,
then you know that you are grown.

Sip your tea like a lady,
cross your knee like a lady,
watch your weight like a lady,
always late like a lady,
carry a purse like a lady,
be a nurse like a lady,
then you know that you are grown.

Kiss a boy like a lady,
oh what joy, like a lady,
when you marry like a lady,
when you tarry like a lady,
have a child like a lady,
meek but wild like a lady,
then you know that you are grown.

Use the phone like a lady,
grunt and groan like a lady,
cook your meals like a lady,

wear high heels like a lady,
keep a house like a lady,
"Eek! A mouse!" like a lady,
then you know you're truly grown.

When old age comes to a lady,
never run from it, lady.
Take it in stride like a lady.
Let it glide like a lady.
Let it come with grace like a lady,
proud with face like a lady.
Then you know you're truly grown.

When you die, die like a lady.
We'll all cry; some like a lady.
"Oh me, oh my," said one lady.
"Oh well good-bye," said another lady.
Glad you didn't tell, dear lady,
that you're going to Hell, dear sweet lady.

December 21, 1974

KING HEROIN

Go,
fly away.
Go fly away, my life.
Fly away, my life,
with King Heroin.

Oh,
go with him.
Go fly with thee tonight.
Fly away, my life,
with King Heroin.

Hypo, my ticket.
Sweet heroin, my boarding pass.
Fly away, my life,
with King Heroin.

Relax and enjoy the trip,
Heroin Hell my new-found home.
Fly away, my life,
with King Heroin.

A cold morgue slab, my destination.
D.O.A., my tagged new name.
Fly away, my life,
with King Heroin.

I found death, by myself,
No one's help, just all alone.
Fly away, my life,
with King Heroin.

He told me on pass-out bills,
"I'll really move my tail for you.
To make your every wish come true.
Take a trip, get real hip.
Welcome to my world!
Fly away your life with me!"
Signed, King Heroin.

"My fee is high to get to the sky.
I already know, just where you want to go.
I'll take you there, have no despair.
Come join the crowd, give me your load,
and I'll put you on that forsaken road
of which there is no return.
All this happiness, no fears, no worry,
all this from me,
for a small fee,
your will power, your mind, your life."

Signed, King Heroin

December 21, 1974

THE STIFF-LEGGED MAN

The stiff-legged man walks silently down the street
with an impish grin slapped across his face.
He is reminiscing upon the good times he had on this very street
while still a youth in his heyday...
how he used to party with his partners...
how he would go-a-gallivanting around with the pretty ladies –
        the ones with the bustling bosoms and the bountiful
        butts...
how he would wine and dine them till the wee hours of the morn-
        ing...
how he used to run the best numbers game in his hood,
staying arm's length away from the police.

He smiles in a contented style
with his little dancing-like shuffle
and continues on his way.
And then, as suddenly as the good memories came,
the bad memories that went along with them...

how his main man got shot...
how the style he once had with the ladies was now a thing of the
        past, non-existent...
No wining and dining had come to him in a long time...
how he always was in debt,
when he couldn't come through with the money for the people
        who played his game...
how that was the reason for him now having a wooden leg,
as a reminder from one of his unsatisfied customers.
And what all he had to go through to maintain that arms-length
        away from the police.

He stops. He grins no more,

but stands in perpetual awe of himself.
Then takes a long, thought-out look at the person he is.
Self-pity, anguish, and despair enwraps this beaten man.
He trembles under the pressure of his bewilderment.
In a futile attempt to lash out, in obsessive anger,
our lone man looks skyward and shouts,
"Is this all of what is to become of me?"

Silence,
with the exception of a lone ambulance wailing somewhere in the
          distance.

The stiff-legged man, regaining his composure, starts his shuffle-
          limp, shuffle-limp dance
down the street again,
shaking his head sadly.

January 26, 1975

WE'VE GOT A BAND

We've got a band that's outta-site,
super together, and dynamite.
Introducing Purple Haze,
to put you into a frenzied craze,
turn your world into a maze, this Purple Haze.

Featuring our latest attraction,
that belongs to a big faction;
she'll make you soar, limp and lame.
Introducing our star, Ms. Lady Cocaine.

And then, to top it off, doing a return engagement,
is Master Herb and his synthesized arrangement.
Cooler than cool, and hotter than flames,
'cause when Master Herb plays, nobody forgets his name.
Just like the Pied Piper, calling all his mice;
you pipe on Master Herb and wind up feeling nice.

This band can appear anytime, anywhere;
to right here, right now, or way over there. So beware!
They keep coming; they keep humming their tune,
like-a "Take me, and you'll die pretty soon."
People boogie to this tune, day in and day out.
People DIE to this tune, that's without a doubt.

Year, this band is together, they know their trade and tool.
And anybody they can get to boogie is a mighty fine fool.
So take care, be aware, Beware!

December 21, 1974

THE CONDUCTOR

As the conductor waves his baton,
I pitch,
I fall.
Lifelessly,
effortlessly,
like a feather
that has been caught up in the transition of west to east winds,
blown by the sirens of the musical.

LET MY LOVE IN

They say you have to see
some real personality;
but that's all right for them.
Still it ain't enough for me.

I read what the eyes can see.

Still another thing.

Muscleman,
I want your body.
I want to love you,
in the sun,
oil on your body.

Come with me,
high in the cascades.
In this way, you'll get to see me,
high in the desert.

Stay with me.
You won't regret.
Take this love,
so deep,
to swim in.

Come to me,
and let my love in.

ABOUT THE AUTHOR

Sybil, (Greek origin) is usually defined as "an oracle or one who can see into the future; Prophetess."

At the tender age of twelve, Sybil sometimes actually felt this way about herself, but never discussed it with anyone. Through some of her poems, as the reader will discover, some of the dates shouldn't line up with the experiences, knowledge, and wisdom that emerges through the narrator's voice. Sybil has been aptly rewarded and terribly chastised at times for sharing her knowledge about a subject. But the need to share was so strong that it drove her to put pencil to paper, sometimes as therapy, as a form or release from being stifled to express her true feelings and observations at other times.

Even as Dr. Ingram evolved over the years with countless accolades and accomplishments to her name, the chastisement arrow still finds her from time to time. Armed with wit, competence, and confidence, Dr. Ingram is now free to professionally respond with sugar-tipped or poison-tipped arrows electronically.

Or still the old school way... putting pencil to paper.